Charley Braunstein and Jewish Tradition

Charley Braunstein and Jewish Tradition

To Adrienne —
Enjoy!
Henry Cohen
xx Ginny Kendall xx

Rabbi Henry Cohen

Illustrations by Virginia Kendall

To order additional copies of this book, contact:
Xlibris Corporation
1-888-795-4274
www.Xlibris.com
Orders@Xlibris.com
47590

CONTENTS

Dedicated to my granddaughter, Tali

"This delightful collection of stories provides a wealth of material for families and synagogues. Rabbi Cohen uses wit and wisdom to transmit Jewish values and important teachings of our tradition. These clever stories will surely engage people of all ages."

—Rabbi Hara Parson, Director of the CCAR Press

"Although I am admittedly biased in my review having had the privilege of growing up listening to these memorable tales, I can objectively vouch for their ability to teach and entertain generations of children of every age, having retold them to my own congregation with great success. Only Henry Cohen can masterfully weave the philosophy of Martin Buber into the fabric of Jewish story telling and the magic of Charley Braunstein."

—Rabbi Bradd Boxman,
a former student of mine who is now rabbi of
Har Sinai Congregation, Owings Mills, MD

"It is amazing how the common humanity of the Peanuts gang resonates with all sectors of our lives. Rabbi Cohen has found these similarities in the youngsters in this book."

—Jean Schulz (Mrs. Charles Schulz)

PREFACE

You all know good old Charlie Brown and his gang. There's Lucy and Linus, Schroeder and Peppermint Patty, and, of course, Snoopy, all created by the brilliant cartoonist, Charles Schulz. Since kids are similar all over the world, it is not surprising that just across town in a Jewish neighborhood, there lives Charley Braunstein. His nemesis is Leila, who lives close enough to always be an annoyance. She also is a pain to her brother, Lazer, on whom she often plays tricks to show him who's boss. Leila is madly in love with Daniel, who was named after pianist-conductor Daniel Barenboim (a prodigy at eight) and whose only love is his piano on which he enjoys playing Beethoven. Another know-it-all is Penina-Pesha, who thinks she knows how to calm down Lazer when he can't find his security blanket. Charley Braunstein's gang celebrate the Jewish holidays, Rosh Hashanah, Yom Kippur, Sukkot, Simchat Torah, Hannukah, Tu B'Shvat, Purim, Pesach, Shavuot, and, of course, Shabbat.

Strange things happen to Charley and his friends on the holidays and Shabbat. There was that Yom Kippur when Leila refused to admit she had ever done anything wrong. One Hanukkah a new kid named Sylvan Sylabbolus moved on the block. Almost every word he said had at least three syllables. Did the gang ever make his life miserable! One Rosh Hashanah the shofar would make only a little peep, and on Purim a grogger (noise maker) wouldn't grog. But the biggest tumult happened when Charley absolutely refused to be a Bar Mitzvah.

On each holiday, Charley and his gang seem to start off on the wrong foot. But they usually end up (with the help of Reb Hayyim) learning what the holiday is all about. By the end of the year, they even have a pretty good idea of what being Jewish is all about.

(After each story, ask yourself: Did I enjoy the story? What is the main meaning of the story? What is the connection between that meaning and my personal life or issues in the society?)

WHEN LAZER LOST HIS BLANKET

Lazer had this blanket. It wasn't the cleanest or the prettiest or the warmest blanket in the house, but it was *his* blanket. He clung to it through thick and thin, especially through thin. It gave him a good feeling inside no matter how things were going on the outside.

One day Lazer lost his blanket. You can imagine how he felt: anxious, nervous, upset and frightened. In fact, he was shaking all over. Poor Lazer, when he lost his blanket, he just fell apart.

Lazer looked everywhere for his blanket, and the gang helped. But nobody—not Leila or Penina-Pesha or Charley Braunstein or Snappy—nobody could find Lazer's blanket. Then Charley said, "If we can't find Lazer's blanket, the least we can do is try to calm him down. The least we can do is to help him be less nervous, less upset, less afraid."

"Leave it to me," said Penina-Pesha. "I'll calm him down." She walked up to Lazer, whacked him on the back and said, "Buck up, Lazer ol' boy. You've got nothing to be upset about. Just say to yourself seven times a day: 'I'm *not* upset . . . I'm *not* nervous . . . I'm NOT afraid. 'I'll guarantee that in three days you won't be afraid at all."

Lazer tried doing what Penina-Pesha said. Seven times a day he repeated, "I'm not upset . . . I'm not nervous . . . I'm not af-f-f-raid." But just saying the words made him even more nervous.

Then Daniel patted Lazer on the back and said, "Penina-Pesha's a boor, a Philistine. I know how to calm you down. Music has charms to soothe the fearful heart. Just listen to this Beethoven sonata and your mind will be at ease."

Daniel began playing the Moonlight Sonata. "V-v-v-very pretty," said Lazer, "but I'm s-s-still n-n-nervous."

Leila tapped Lazer on the head and said, "Obviously this is a case that calls for professional counseling. Come to my office tomorrow after school." The next day Lazer went to Leila's office. (It was actually a lemonade stand but the lemonade sign had been replaced by a sign reading "Psychiatric Help—10 cents) Leila said: "Tell me, Lazer old buddy, what are you afraid of?"

"I don't know," said Lazer.

"Well, I'll tell you," said Leila. "You're afraid of going to Kindergarten next year."

"But I *want* to go to Kindergarten next year," said Lazer.

"You just think you want to go," said Leila, "but you're really scared and I'll tell you why. When you were two years old, your parents left you with a baby sitter, and she fell asleep and in the middle of the night you woke up and cried, and the sitter didn't hear you, and you cried and cried 'til your parents came home, and ever since that time when the baby sitter went to sleep, you haven't let go of your blanket."

Lazer scratched his head. "But what does that have to do with my being afraid to go to Kindergarten?"

"Aha," said Leila, "NOW you're afraid that when you go to Kindergarten and something happens to make you cry, the teacher—like that baby sitter—won't be there to help you. That's why you're afraid of Kindergarten and that's why you want your blanket!"

"You've gotta be kidding," said Lazer.

"Don't interrupt," snapped Leila. "Now that you realize the reason why you're afraid, you don't have to be afraid anymore. Now that you understand that all your fears go back to that baby-sitter who fell asleep, you can forget about your old blanket! That'll be ten cents, please." Lazer paid Leila the ten cents, but he was still upset, nervous and afraid.

Then it was that Charley Braunstein said, "I know what let's do. Let's make a Shabbat for Lazer. "So the next Friday evening, all the gang came together at Charley's house for a "Shabbos-dikke" dinner.

Penina-Pesha lit the candles. After singing the blessing, she said, "These candles glow with the warmth of love we feel for Lazer."

"For me?" asked Lazer.

"Yes, for you," shouted everybody.

SHABBAT TABLE

Then Charley sang the *kiddush*, the blessing over the wine, and he added: "As we drink this wine, this symbol of joy, we wish for Lazer all the happiness in the world."

Then Lazer's mother, who with his father had been invited to the Shabbat dinner, brought him a big bowl of chicken soup, smiled and said, "So eat already." Everyone had a delicious meal. After eating, they sang songs like "Shabbat Shalom" (Sabbath peace) and "Yaaseh Shalom" (Let there be peace), and Lazer began to feel sort of peaceful inside.

After the singing, the gang went to services in the synagogue. Lazer noticed that Rabbi Hayyim was wearing a prayer shawl. His father told him it was a *tallit*, but to Lazer it looked a lot like his blanket. He thought to himself: I guess I'm not the only one who needs security.

Prayers were said and sung, and then the Rabbi began his sermon. He seemed to be looking at Lazer when he said: "If ever you need a helping hand, you'll find one: at the end of your arm. You can do more for yourself than you think. But," continued the Rabbi, "for all of us there comes a time when we need somebody else's hand—if only to touch, if only to make us feel somebody cares. Look around you this evening and think of all those people who love you, who care for you, who will be there when you need them. A man named Martin Buber once said that between you and the people you love, you can find God."

Lazer looked around. He wondered if God really was there—between himself and his mother . . . between himself and his father . . . between himself and his good friend, Charley Braunstein. At the end of the service, everyone sang, 'Ayn Kelohaynu.' (There is none like God), Lazer's father and mother kissed him and said "Shabbat shalom" (a Sabbath of peace) Even Leila kissed him. And Charley smiled.

For some reason. Lazer was not upset anymore. He went home feeling good inside. He felt that people liked him, and he even liked himself. That night when Lazer got into bed, he was just about to fall asleep when his toes touched something. You guessed it: his security blanket! Lazer laughed, "I don't need YOU anymore." He rolled the blanket into a ball and started to throw it out of the window. Then he stopped and thought for a moment. He unrolled the blanket, folded it very carefully and put it in the bottom of his dresser drawer. Softly he said to himself: "Just for emergencies." Then immediately he fell into a deep sleep.

CHARLEY BRAUNSTEIN
AND THE BABY SHOFAR

On Rosh Hashana a man known as the Baal Tekiah blows the shofar: Tekiah, Shevarim, Teruah, Tekiah G'dolah. In Charley Braunstein's synagogue there were three shofars: a Papa shofar, a Mama shofar and a tiny baby shofar. The Papa shofar made a powerful sound and was supposed to wake up the conscience of every congregant and remind him or her what he or she had done wrong during the past year: Tekiah! (a straight unbroken sound that ends abruptly)

SHOFAR (Ram's Horn)

The Mama shofar, with its up and down sound was more comforting. It seemed to say: You should really feel sorry for the bad things you did last year. Then maybe you won't feel so guilty: Shevarim! (three broken sounds)!

But the baby shofar made a staccato like sound: Teruah (nine trills). But this year the baby shofar made no sound at all. Many of the large men tried to get a sound from the baby shofar, but nothing came out. Reb Hayyim was troubled. He told the congregants that unless the baby shofar is sounded, then most of the people will not have made *complete repentance.*

But what did the rabbi mean by complete repentance? The rabbi explained that only someone who had made complete repentance could get a sound out of the baby shofar. He told the congregation that maybe one of the children could get a sound out of the baby shofar. Maybe one of the children had made complete repentance.

Guess who was the first to raise her hand. That's right: Leila. She told the rabbi that she had made complete repentance. "I read every prayer and I prayed louder than any other kid in the shul. I read every word correctly and I finished each prayer before anyone else. So the rabbi let Leila try. She blew and blew but just a tiny squeak came out of the shofar.

Then Lazer raised his hand. "Rabbi, I made complete repentance. I not only read the prayers but I really felt sorry for the wrongs that I had done. Last week Leila picked on me that I got so mad that I started kicking Charley's dog, Snappy. I really made him yelp. Now I realize how wrong it was for me to beat up on Snappy just because Leila beat up on me. The rabbi let Lazer try. He blew and blew but, again, just a tiny squeak.

Then Charley Braunstein raised his hand and said: "Rabbi, last month a new family moved on the block. They have a son who stutters. All the gang made fun of him, and I did too. We chased him down the block and he ran home crying. Well, yesterday before Rosh Hashanah I felt sorry for what I had done. So I went over to his house and told him I was sorry, and I invited him to my house to play. We became friends, and I brought him to services today." The Rabbi let Charley try and sure enough out of the baby shofar came nine staccato notes, loud and clear. The rabbi then said Tekiah G'dolah, and for the first time out of the baby shofar came a very long sound that ended only when Charley ran out of breath.

The Rabbi said: "Do you know why Charley could blow the baby shofar? Because he had made complete repentance. He not only said and sang the prayers. He not only felt sorry for what he had done that was wrong, but he actually apologized and he made things right. In Judaism we pray and we promise, but the most important thing is what we do! So ask yourself: What have I actually done this year to make right something that was wrong? Maybe you did it at home. Maybe in the neighborhood. Maybe at school. Maybe you heard about some suffering somewhere in the world and you gave a contribution to those who are trying to make the suffering stop. I believe if you think long and hard enough, you will be able to remember something you did to make a difference for good in the world. Then, and only then, will you be able to sound the baby shofar."

LEILA SAYS I'M SORRY

The whole gang went to services on Yom Kippur. The Rabbi explained that Yom Kippur means "Day of Atonement" and Atonement means that people should be "at one" with each other and with God. But Charley and his friends still didn't understand. After a while the Rabbi asked them to join in a sing-song prayer that began "*Al het . . .*"—"for the sin we sinned before Thee." He explained that this prayer should remind them of all the things they had done during the past year that were wrong. When they said this prayer, they were supposed to feel sorry for the wrongs they had done.

So Charley, Lazer, Daniel and Penina-Pesha all repeated the words of the prayer: We are sorry for all the times we lied . . . for all the times we cheated . . . for all the times we played unfairly . . . for all the times we did not help when we could have helped. Everyone in the gang said the prayer that is, except Leila. She just stood there looking superior not saying a word.

After services the gang gathered round Leila and Charley asked her, "Why didn't you say the *Al Het* with the rest of us?"

Leila answered, "Why should I? I haven't done anything to feel sorry for."

Charley answered, "What about last week when you held the football for me to kick and you promised not to drop it like you do every year and

I believed you, and you dropped it, and I fell flat on my back? Shouldn't you feel sorry for doing that to me?"

"Whatzamatta, Charley Braunstein, can't you take a joke? I'm not gonna feel sorry for having a little harmless fun."

Then Lazer said: "What about the time you hid my security blanket and wouldn't tell me where it was? You know I fall apart without my blanket."

`Leila snapped back: "I took your blanket away for your own good . . . so you could learn to be independent . . . so you could learn to stand on your own two feet instead of always clinging to that dumb blanket."

Charley spoke up again: "What about all those times you called Lazer or me stupid. You know it's wrong to hurt the feelings of others."

Leila didn't blink an eye. "On those days when I called you names, I'd had a really rough time at school. The teacher had picked on me . . . the older kids pushed me around. I couldn't get back at them and I had to take my anger out on somebody. You and Lazer happened to be around. You should understand that I was under so much pressure that I couldn't help myself. I'm sure not going to blame myself for something I couldn't help doing."

Suddenly Snappy started barking. Lazer translated: "Snappy is reminding you of the time you gave him a box of fleas for his birthday."

"Oh," said Leila, "Snappy is only a dog." With that Leila stuck her nose up in the air and walked away.

After Leila had left, the gang went into a huddle to figure out how they could teach Leila a lesson. How could they teach her to admit that she had done some things that were wrong? How could they make Leila say, "I'm sorry"? They talked and talked and were getting nowhere when Daniel banged on his piano and said: "I have a plan. It can't miss. Just be at my house in five days early on the morning of Sukkot."

The gang knew that Sukkot was a happy thanksgiving holiday when they had their meals in a three-sided booth (called a sukkah) covered with leafy branches, fruits and vegetable. They also knew that Leila was madly in love with Daniel but that Daniel wouldn't give her the time of day, because he was in love with his piano. They wondered what Daniel had up his sleeve.

After Yom Kippur was over, Daniel went over to Leila's house, set up his piano beneath her window and began playing Beethoven's Moonlight Sonata. Leila came out on her balcony in her nightgown and thought, "How romantic." As he played, Daniel cried, "Leila, my love, I don't know what has come over me but I have a burning yearning churning deep inside of me. I must meet you five days from now at midnight under the sukkah."

Leila cooed, "I'll be there." She was so excited. At last Daniel had seen the light. At last he realized how lovable she was. For the next five days Leila was so thrilled that she went around singing: "Shine on, shine on Sukkah moon, up in the sky I ain't had no lovin' since Purim, Hannuka, the Fourth of July . . ." Leila was on cloud seven.

Came the night of Sukkot. Leila dressed up in her Sukkot best and went to meet Daniel under the sukkah. Horror of horrors! Daniel wasn't there! All Leila found in the middle of the sukkah was a big pumpkin, and in the pumpkin was a note: 'I WOULDN'T MEET YOU ANYWHERE ANYPLACE ANY TIME IF YOU WERE THE LAST GIRL IN THE WORLD. WHAT I THINK OF YOU I CAN SAY IN ONE WORD; BLAAAHH.'

Leila was crushed. She hardly ever cried, but this time she couldn't help herself. The tears just came. After she had cried a while, she got angry: "That no-good Daniel! How could he do such a mean thing?" Early that morning she marched over to Daniel's house and found him serenely playing the piano. She banged her fist on the piano and screamed "Daniel, how could you do such a mean thing?"

Daniel answered: "Like you said to Charley when you dropped the football and he fell on his back: it was only harmless fun; can't you take a joke?"

"Like you said to Lazer when you took away his security blanket, I was only trying to help you stand on your own two feet, to make you less dependent on me. It was for your own good."

"And like you said to Charley and Lazer when you called them stupid: 'I had such a rough day at school that I couldn't help myself. I had to take out my frustration on someone.'"

"And like you said when you gave Snappy a box of fleas, you're only a dog!"

Leila was even more furious. "I'm sick and tired of your excuses. It was still mean and being mean is wrong!"

Just at that moment, the whole gang came out from hiding. "You're right," said Charley, "We can always find excuses for the things we did that were wrong. But we should admit, especially on Yom Kippur, that at times we do act in ways that hurt people. Whatever explanations we make, we still have a choice between right and wrong. We should still feel sorry for making others unhappy. And we should try not to do such things again."

Leila, for the first time ever, did not look so superior. She said, "I guess you're right, gang. I guess I am s-s-s-" She had a hard time getting the word out but finally she said it: "I guess I am s-s-s-sorry for some of the things I've done."

Then Daniel gave her a kiss on the cheek. "I don't hate you," he said. "I was just trying to teach you what Yom Kippur is all about."

WHEN THE SUKKAH FELL ON LEILA

It was the eve of Sukkot and Charley Braunstein and the gang went to the family service in their synagogue, which they called Bet David, the House of David. They looked forward to the waving of the lulav (palm branch) and good old Reb Hayyim's Sukkot story. But this year Reb Hayyim had a very serious face. He told the children and their parents, "I just don't feel up to telling an entertaining Sukkot story. I'm too upset, worried, depressed."

"What's your problem?" asked Charley. "This is a happy holiday when we enjoy the fruits and vegetables of the field and thank God for all the good things in our lives. Cheer up, Reb, and tell us a story."

"Sorry," said Reb Hayyim, "but I'm too frustrated and angry at what people are doing to God's good earth. I'm afraid that many years from now, life on earth will be miserable for your children or their children or their children. The way we're using up our oil and polluting the air and making the earth so warm that there will be more storms and large portions of land will just disappear—I just get so discouraged."

"Hold on," said Charley, "What do you mean we're making the earth too warm. I've heard about global warming, but can you explain it so kids can understand it."

"Good question," said Reb Hayyim. "Scientists are convinced that the earth is heated by light waves from the sun. Some of that solar energy is good and warms the earth, but some must be sent back into space or else the earth will continue getting warmer, and we are making matters worse."

"I don't understand," said Charley.

"Well," said the Rabbi, "it is complicated, but you should have learned in school that the earth is protected by a layer of atmosphere and that atmosphere is getting dangerously warm because carbon dioxide and other gasses that WE send into space trap the radiation that should escape the atmosphere so that the earth remains at a livable temperature. If that doesn't happen, the ice near the north and south poles will melt, the oceans will become warmer, large tracts of land will disappear, storms will become stronger and more frequent. Animals that depend on a moderate temperature will disappear. And the way we are using up oil will mean in future generations people won't be able to drive around in cars. If we don't change our way of living, the future will be a nightmare."

"How do you know all this?" asked Leila. "You're just a rabbi."

"You'll understand when you are able to read Al Gore's book, *An Inconvenient Truth*," or see the movie."

"So what can we do about it?" asked Lazer. "We're just kids."

"Never thought you'd ask," said Reb Hayyim. "During the week of Sukkot you can begin performing *mitzvot teva*, commandments of nature. To keep the level of carbon dioxide down, you can let yourself be driven as little as possible; walk more. Use your bicycle. You can separate bottles, cans and trash and have them recycled. You can cut down on your use of paper bags, because paper comes from trees, and trees inhale carbon dioxide and the more trees you cut down, the more carbon dioxide goes into the atmosphere. The rabbis said that God told Adam: 'This is the last world I will create. Take care of it, for there won't be another.'"

While the gang was having a snack in the sukkah, Charley said, "I think Reb Hayyim is right. Our parents keep telling us to clean up our rooms. I say to them: "Clean up the world."

The gang nodded in agreement, all expect Leila, who snapped: "Who cares what happens 100, 200, 300 or 500 years from now. I'm not gonna be here."

"That's a terrible attitude," said Charley. "Didn't you hear what the Rabbi said?"

"He's only a rabbi," said Leila. "I want to hear from a Higher Authority." Suddenly there was thunder and lightning, powerful winds and a torrential rain. The kids ran into the synagogue, but not Leila. "Who's afraid of a little thunder storm." As she munched on her apple, a large branch from the roof of the sukkah fell and hit Leila on the head and she drifted into dreamland.

Leila dreamed she was flying through time and space. The wind was whirling about her and she saw this figure sitting on a giant blintz. He looked like Reb Hayyim and he cried, "See, my pretty, so you don't care what happens a hundred years from today . . . we'll see . . . heh, heh, heh."

Finally Leila came down to earth and she could hardly believe her eyes. She was lying beneath a withered old tree that had not a single leaf. There was a gray smog in the air that made her eyes burn and the smell was awful. A man appeared dressed in baggy clothes and wearing a gas mask. "Stu's the name . . . the zoo's my game."

"Tell me, Mr. Zoo-man," said Leila, "Where on or off earth am I?"

"You're just a few miles outside of Filthydelphia, the City of Smotherly Love. It used to be called 'Philadelphia, the City of Brotherly Love,' but that was five hundred years before the earth got so rotten because there was no place to put the trash, not even underground."

Leila grumbled, "Yech, what a miserable world. How could you let all this happen?"

"How could WE let it happen? It's not our fault. Way back in the 1990's, our ancestors said: 'Who cares what happens to the world after we're no longer here? So they cut down all the forests, used up all the oil, polluted the water, poisoned the air—all because they didn't care about anyone but themselves."

"That was awfully mean," said Leila, but she felt funny inside as though maybe she had done something wrong.

"Cheer up," said Stu. "Let me show you our zoo. It's only ten miles."

"So where's your car,?" asked Leila.

"You must be kidding," said Stu. "Cars are only for emergencies. But there are lots of ways to travel: roller skates, walking, and if you can afford it, a bicycle."

"I'll bike, if you don't mind," said Leila, so they rented a ten-speed rent-a-bike from Avis and off they went up and down the hills. Leila was huffing and puffing, 'til finally they came to the zoo. When Stu asked Leila what she would like to see first, she said the elephants. So Stu took her to a large cage in which there was a giant picture of an elephant. "Who wants to see a picture," cried Leila. "Where are the elephants?"

"There aren't anymore," said Stu. "They were all killed so people could use the ivory from their tusks to make house decorations. Would you like to throw some peanuts at the picture?"

"That's not funny," said Leila. Then they came to the giraffe cage. Again a picture, but no live giraffe. Stu explained that when the trees in the jungle were cut down or burned, the giraffes did not have enough to eat, so they died. "So what do you have in the zoo that's alive?"

'Right this way," said Stu and they came to a cage that had about a dozen mice. "Somehow mice find enough to eat."

"I've seen and smelled enough," said Leila. "How do I get out of here. I want to go back to Philadelphia."

"No problem," said Stu. "Our zoo has a sukkah. If you make seven circles in the sukkah, and then sing a song that tells why you want to return, then you will."

SUKKAH

Leila went into the sukkah and began to sing:
How I want to go back to
A world where skies are blue
Where lots of animals are in the zoo
Where the air won't make you cough
Or smell like a piggy's trough
Please somebody take me off
And send me home to my friends
How I long to see some trees
And enjoy the autumn breeze
Send me back to Philly, PLEASE

Leila felt woozy, fainted and when she opened her eyes, who was standing over her with a big smile?—Charley Braunstein. Daniel was playing on the piano Beethoven's Moonlight Sonata. Lazer even offered her his security blanket, and Snappy barked with joy.

"You've been out for a whole hour," said Charley.

"No," said Leila, "I've been out for five hundred years but now I'm back and I tell you that Reb Hayyim was right. We had better start taking better care of our world cause if we don't—one day it will be total disaster for boys and girls like you and me."

"But what can we do besides recycling and walking more?" asked Lazer.

"We could write our congress persons," said Charley. "But what should we write him or her to do?"

Reb Hayyim had been listening to the whole conversation and he suggested six steps that Al Gore said we could do: 1) We can make more efficient use of electricity in heating and cooling systems, lighting appliances and electronic equipment; 2) We can design buildings that use much less energy than they do now; 3) We can make cars that run on less gas and put more hybrid and fuel-cell cars on the road (that means cars that run on both electricity and gas and on vegetation like corn); 4) We can design cities that have better transit systems; 5) We can rely more on renewable energy technologies like the wind; 6) We can do a better job of storing excess carbon from power plants.

"We should all know, especially on Sukkot, the danger that threatens our earth, air and water, and we should know that if we don't do something, it may be too late. So this Sukkot, let us not only thank God for this wonderful world but let's do our part in making sure that this beautiful world is here for many years to come."

And the gang said: "Amen,"

WHAT'S TRUE IN THE TORAH

Charley Braunstein and the gang all went to Simchat Torah services. They really enjoyed the parade when they followed the Torahs around the synagogue, singing and dancing. After the Torah parade (Hakafot), Reb Hayyim chanted the very end of one Torah and the very beginning of another Torah. He explained that this was to show that learning Torah should never stop.

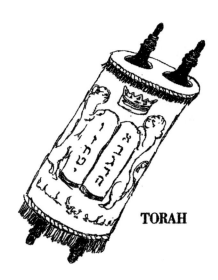

TORAH

Because the Torah reading was the more serious part of the service, the gang sat quietly while the Rabbi chanted about the creation of the world and the first human beings, man and woman. A member of the congregation translated as the Rabbi chanted. Most of the kids were not paying too much attention, but Leila was. Leila listened closely as the translator read about the world being created in just six days, about how even before the sun and stars there was a first light. Then the earth was created and after the earth was formed, according to the Torah, the sun and moon were created, and how on the sixth day human beings were created, one male and one female. (In the second chapter they are called Adam and Eve).

Just as the Torah reading was finished, Leila cried out: "I don't believe the part about God creating the world in six days. That contradicts everything I learned in science." Well, the congregation was shocked. Just imagine, an eight year old girl interrupting the chanting of the Torah and saying the Torah was not true. What a disgrace! What a shanda! What hutzpa! The shamas was ready to throw Leila out of the synagogue, when good old Reb Hayyim raised his hand for quiet.

"Leila raises a very important question," said Reb Hayyim. "Just what IS true in the Torah? The Torah begins with stories we call myths and these myths may not be word for word accurate, but they do contain a very special kind of truth."

"Whadaya mean?" asked Leila. "Either the story is true or it isn't."

Reb Hayyim smiled and said, "Myths are not that simple. You see, long ago before there was science, our ancestors asked very difficult questions about how the world and the people in it came to be. They came up with very imaginative answers, even if they were not always according to modern science. For instance, they were mistaken in believing that the earth was created before the sun."

"So," said Leila, "why bother reading these stories if they contradict science?"

"Because," said Reb Hayyim. We do not look to the Torah for science. We look to the Torah to teach us how to live better happier, more peaceful lives. For example, when the Torah says that the entire universe was created by one God, this means that God could make laws that are true all over the world."

"What kind of laws?" asked Charley.

Reb Hayyim answered: "All over the world, for seeds to grow into flowers, there must be sun and rain, and all over the world, for children to grow into happy caring adults, they must be given a lot of love. That is a very important truth."

"Maybe so," said Leila, "but what about that part when God created the first man and woman? How do we know there really was an Adam and Eve?"

Charley joined in: "Leila, you're missing the point. I think that when the Torah says Adam was the first human being, what it really means is that since we are all descended from Adam, we are all related to each other and we should treat each other with respect, as members of the same family."

"Very good," said the Rabbi. "When you children sang the Shema, you were saying that we are all united by certain needs and wishes we have in common. What do you think we have in common just because we're human?"

Penina-Pesha piped up: "We all like sports."

Reb Hayyim: "Maybe not everybody, but we do like to enjoy ourselves."

Lazer, clinging to his blanket, said, "We all want to be s-s-s-secure. We don't want to be n-n-nervous all the time."

"You're right," said Reb Hayyim, "and what do we need to help us feel secure?"

`Charley said, "We all need somebody to love us."

"You're right, Charley," said the Rabbi, "and one day you children will learn that we not only need to BE loved but we need to find someone whom we can love."

Daniel chimed in: "I need to play the piano."

Reb Hayyim said, "We don't all need to play the piano, but we do need to express ourselves, to make the most of our talents."

Charley said: "We forgot one thing: We all have problems. My baseball team never wins. I have too much homework. Sometimes the gang thinks I'm weird."

Reb Hayyim replied: "You're not the only one with problems, Charley. I have to think of something different and interesting to say every Friday night. We all have to struggle to make it from day to day."

Leila: "Sure we have problems, but we should be able to solve them."

Reb Hayyim: "Yes, Leila, we can solve our problems with the help of family and friends and with God's help."

Leila barked: "What does God have to do with it?"

Reb Hayyim: "Each of you children has within you the power to grow. You did not create this power. The power comes from God. No matter how difficult life seems to be, God has given you the power to grow in confidence. Your mind will grow in knowledge. Your heart will grow in love."

Charley looked thoughtful. "I think Reb Hayyim is saying that if God the creator is one, this means that in some ways we are all one. We all share a common humanity. We all need to enjoy life, to feel secure, to be loved and to love, to struggle to make it from day to day and to grow toward happiness. If we all have these needs, then I don't feel so lonely any more."

Reb Hayyim remarked: "Charley, you just learned one truth we find in the Torah, but as you continue in Religious School, you'll learn many more truths in the Torah. For example, the Torah says: 'Love your neighbor as yourself.' Also we should not tell lies (like bearing 'false witness.') Just because others are doing something wrong, you should not go along with the crowd just to be popular. *Kadosh*, or holy, means being set aside for a higher purpose. In weekday school you'll learn about science (and that's very important) but in Religious School you'll learn how we can live better happier lives and how we can find the ways of pleasantness and the paths of peace."

Leila muttered: "Well, I guess there is something true in the Torah after all."

SYLVAN SYLLABOLUS CELEBRATES HANUKKAH

One bright day in November a new kid moved in on Charley Braunstein's block. His name was Sylvan Syllabolus. Sylvan was in love with syllables. He would never use one syllable when he could use two or three. For example, he would never say, "That was a good meal." Instead he would say, "That culinary concoction was a delectable Epicurean delight." He would never say to Charley: "Let's walk down the street to see a movie. Instead he would say, "Let's perambulate down the boulevard to the cinema." Even when playing he would never say, "Throw the ball." Instead he would cry out: "Project the spheroid through the atmosphere."

As you might have guessed, Sylvan was not the most popular kid on the block. In fact, Charley's friends thought that he was weird: not only did he use such big words but he dressed in the strangest way: he always wore a coat and tie. And he was learning to play the violin.

The kids on the block made fun of Sylvan. Leila gave him the nickname Silly, and the kids would often shout at him: "Silly Syllabolus, don't be a snobolus." Leila would lead the shouting. Lazer would twirl his blanket in the air. Snappy would bark with fiendish glee. Only Charley Braunstein stood silent and watched.

After the gang had made fun of Sylvan Syllabolus for a few weeks, it was time for Hanukkah. Leila called the kids together and said, "I have a great idea. Let's invite Silly to a costume Hanukkah party at Charley's house, only there won't be a party. Sylvan received an invitation in the mail; he dressed up like a dreidl and spun down the street just as Charley and his family were lighting the Hanukkah candles.

"No party here," said Charley. Sylvan realized the kids had played a joke on him. Without saying a word, he walked home.

The next day in Religious School, Reb Hayyim was talking to the kids about Hanukkah. But Sylvan wasn't there. He had told his mother he had an upset stomach. But the rest of gang was there when Reb Hayyim asked the class: "Who here knows what Hanukkah is all about?"

"I know," said Lazer. "Hanukkah is about lighting candles, eating latkes and getting presents, for each of eight nights."

MENORAH

"Sounds like fun," said the Rabbi, "but is that really what Hanukkah is all about?"

"Oh no," said Leila. "Hanukkah is about the Maccabees. The Jews were being pushed around by that mean Antiochus, who wouldn't even let them practice their religion. Then Judah and his brothers took to the hills followed by many Jews. They attacked the army of Antiochus. They really clobbered them: zap, zing, a-a-a-a-a-boom! What a great victory. Those Maccabees really laid it on those Greeks, and that's what Hanukkah is all about: beating the enemy."

JUDAH MACCABEE

"Sorry," said the Rabbi. "You're wrong for a couple of reasons. First, Antiochus was off to the East fighting the Parthians. Judah did win a military victory. Then he and his brothers made peace with the Greeks and were given religious freedom. But why do you think the Maccabees revolted?"

"I know," said Charley. "Antiochus wanted everyone to be just like he was: a Greek who had the Greek religion and went to Greek gymnasiums and ate Greek food. He couldn't stand for anybody to be different: to have their own tradition. The Jews had to fight to protect their right to be different."

"Very good," said the Rabbi. "You're beginning to see what Hanukkah is all about. It's about the right of every person to live his or her own way of life so long as others are not hurt. It's about the right of a person to have what ever religion he or she chooses. It's about the right for everyone to think and talk and dress in his or her own way. Children, Hanukkah is about being yourself, and letting others be themselves without making fun of them if they are different from you."

Suddenly the class became very quiet. Can you guess what they were thinking? That's right. They were thinking about Sylvan Syllabolus and how they had made his life miserable just because he used big words and dressed with a coat and tie and played the violin. Charley broke the silence. "I have an idea, gang. Let's have a real Hanukkah party, a party in honor of our new neighbor, Sylvan Syllabolus."

"Great idea," said Lazer. Even Leila went along. So all the kids went to Sylvan's house. They said they were sorry for what they had done and invited Sylvan to a real party. So Sylvan came to the party. He brought his violin and played the Draydl Song while the gang swung their partners. While Lazer was munching on a latke, he asked Sylvan, "Do you think you could help me with my English homework?"

"Glad to," said Sylvan. Charley turned to Snappy and said: "I guess that's what Hanukkah's all about."

Who should appear as an unexpected guest but Reb Hayyim. He told the kids: "If you would bring the spirit of Hanukkah into your lives, you will never pick on other people just because they seem odd or different. That's the beginning of prejudice. When newcomers who are different move into the neighborhood or into your classroom, go out of your way to be friendly. And if your ideas and interests are different from those of others, stand up for them."

Leila had been sitting in the corner writing a poem which she read to the gang:

I'm oh so glad that other folks are not just like me

If everyone were just the same how boring life would be

How dull if people everywhere had the same color hair or skin Or if every fan throughout the land wanted the same football team to win.

And if everybody looked and talked alike and thought the same way too; How could I tell the difference between him and her and you?

So let's give to others freedom, the right to choose their way

When nations learn this simple truth, we'll see a brighter day.

AND THAT'S WHAT HANUKKAH IS ALL ABOUT!

WHAT TU B'SHVAT IS ALL ABOUT:
BUB THE SHRUB

Reb Hayyim announced that there would be a special Tu B'Shvat service to celebrate the birthday of the trees. "That's ridiculous," said Leila. "Trees don't have birthdays."

Charley Braunstein said: "Let's go to the service. Maybe the Rabbi will explain what Tu B'Sh'vat is all about."

So the gang went to the synagogue and listened to the Rabbi say: "Tu B'Shvat means the 15th of the Hebrew month of Sh'vat. According to tradition, that's when trees came into being. It usually falls in January or February (a cold time for trees to be created) but in Israel signs of Spring come early."

Leila interrupted: "But the Torah doesn't mention a new year for trees."

"You're right," said Reb Hayyim, "but some rabbis considered how important trees are: they keep the ground from becoming a desert. They provide a place where many kinds of animals can live. They prevent too much carbon dioxide from being trapped in the atmosphere and so slow down global warming"

"Yes, but," Lazer said, "are there any good stories about trees?"

The Rabbi thought for a while and said, "the Torah is called 'a tree of life to those who hold fast to it.' My favorite tree story is based on a midrash, a rabbinic commentary."

"So tell it already," said Penina-Pesha.

"I will," said the Rabbi, "but only if you'll tell me what the story means."

"No problem,:" said Leila.

The Rabbi began: "Long long ago a man named Max went into the forest. Max looked at all the trees and cried: 'My name is Max . . . I need wood for my ax'

"Max already had a bright sharp and shiny blade, but he needed a piece of wood that he could attach to the blade. Then he would have an ax. Again he called out to the trees in the forest: 'My name is Max . . . I need wood for my ax.'

"The strongest tree in the forest was a big thick oak. Its branches stretched so far that they pushed all the other trees away. The oak looked down at Max and said: 'No way! If you try to take my branches I will pick you up and throw you high in the sky.' And the oak's branches dipped down and Max became scared and ran to another part of the forest.

"Max ran until he came to a cedar. The cedar was the tallest tree in the forest. Max looked up to the top of the tree and cried: 'Please, Mr.

Cedar, I would really like some of your wood so I could make a handle for my ax.'

"'Forget it,' said the cedar. 'If you touch me, I'll tell the birds in my branches to throw their eggs on you.'

"Max moved away from the cedar as quickly as he could. He found himself next to a straight pine tree. 'Please, Mr. Pine, all I want is a piece of wood to make a handle for my ax.'

"'Sorry,' said the pine. 'If you lay a finger on me, I'll stick you with my needles and throw my pine cones on your head.'

"Max became angry and started shouting: 'If one of you trees don't give me some of your wood for my ax, I'll start a fire and burn down the forest.'

"So the trees put their branches together to figure out what to do. The pine said: 'Max is bluffing. He would never set fire to the forest. The fire would spread and burn down his own house at the edge of the forest.' But all the other trees were afraid that Max would really start a forest fire.

"Then the oak came up with an idea: 'Let's give Max the smallest tree in the forest, Bub the Shrub. The oak said: 'Bub, baby, we have decided that Max should pull you out of the ground so he can use your wood for the ax he is making.'

"'Oh no,' cried Bub the Shrub. 'Don't let Max pull me out of the ground. I warn you. You'll be sorry.'

"But the big trees just laughed and said to Max: 'Do whatever you want with Bub the Shrub. He can't hurt you.'" So Max grabbed the thin trunk of Bub the Shrub and pulled and pulled until Bub was completely out of the ground. Then Max took Bub's trunk home and made it into a handle for his ax.

"The next week Max went back into the forest with his ax. He said to himself: 'I need lots of wood to build a barn behind my house.' So he started chopping down the trees. First he chopped down the big thick oak. Then he chopped down the tall cedar. Then he chopped down the straight pine.

"As the big trees in the forest were falling, they cried to each other, 'If only we had not been so mean to Bub the Shrub! If only we had not picked on the smallest tree! If only we would have stood up for each other! If only we would have been united with all our fellow-trees, then we would not be falling dowwwn noooow . . .'"

"So, kids," said the Rabbi, "What does the story tell us?"

Daniel started playing on the piano, "I think that I shall never see a poem as lovely as a tree."

"Let's get serious," said Charley, "Obviously the story is telling us that if the big and powerful pick on the small and weak, even the strongest will fall."

"That's right," said the Rabbi. "It's been said that a society is judged by how it treats its weakest members. If we sacrifice the helpless so we can be protected, eventually we will suffer, maybe even be destroyed."

Charley asked "Do you mean that if we prevent the poorest from living a better life, then eventually we all will have a worse life."

"That's the general idea," said the Rabbi. "The poor, the homeless, the unskilled, we do need them. We need them not to be a threat to us or to be a drain on our resources. We need their talents and abilities to make this a happier nation for all its people."

THE OAK & THE SHRUB

"But what does this have to do with the Jews?" snapped Penina-Pesha.

The Rabbi replied. "I'm glad you asked. Just think of the history of the Jewish people. At times they were sacrificed, chopped down. But do you know what eventually happened to the people who stood around and watched the Jews getting chopped down, whether in Russia or in Germany? They, themselves, got chopped down. In other words the choppers got chopped. For scapegoating, picking on the little guy, this is a sign of weakness. And when a society resorts to picking on its Bubs, that entire society is in trouble. So remember Bub the Shrub. We're all trees in the forest. Let's stick together, because we do need each other. And if this argument from self-interest does not convince you, let's care for each other, because it's the right thing to do."

Charley said, "So that's what Tu B'Shvat is all about."

And the gang said: "Amen."

THE GROGGY GROGGER

A grogger is a noise maker that sounds like a lion gargling. The raspy raucous noise of hundreds of groggers fills the synagogue on Purim everytime the rabbi reads the name of Haman from the *Megilla.* The *Megilla* is the scroll on which is written the story of Esther, the Jewish queen of Persia who foiled the plot of the wicked Haman to destroy all the Jews in the kingdom.

The week before Purim Charley Braunstein and his gang came home from Religious School with their groggers. The teachers wanted them to practice grogger-twirling so they would be ready for Haman. So Leila, Lazer, Daniel and Penina-Pesha all were twirling their groggers, tuning up for the *Megilla* reading. The last to come home was Charley, but when he twirled his grogger, it wouldn't grog. He tried and tried. Not a sound!

"What's the matter, Charley Braunstein?" asked Leila in her mocking voice. "Don't you even know how to twirl a grogger?"

GROGGER

Lazer, clinging to his blanket asked with some sympathy "Are you feeling inadequate, Charley?"

All Charley could answer was: "Nobody's perfect."

The gang, led by Leila, kept making fun of him, so Charley said to Leila. "You think you're so smart, You twirl my grogger."

"Glad to," said Leila. She took Charley's grogger and twirled and twirled, but nothing happened.

"Let me have that grogger, kid" said Penina-Pesha. She gave it her best wind-up. Still, no sound.

That's when Lazer said: "You know, Charley Braunstein, you've got a groggy grogger."

Then Charley got another idea. "Let's take my grogger to the Rabbi. He'll fix it, because our Rabbi really knows his groggers.

So the next day after school, the whole gang went with Charley to the Rabbi and showed him the grogger. The Rabbi looked at the grogger for a long time and said in a deep wizard-of-Oz type voice. "This is a magic grogger. It was made many years ago by Rabbi Loewe of Prague and it has come to be known as the Praguer Grogger."

"THE PRAGUER GROGGER!" cried Lazer, his eyes bulging in disbelief.

"Yes," said the Rabbi. "This is the Praguer Grogger," and he continued, "the Praguer Grogger will grog only for someone who really understands the meaning of Purim."

"There's only one thing to do, gang," said Charley. "We better learn what Purim is all about. Then maybe we can get some noise out of the groggy Praguer grogger."

The next day in Religious School, the teachers told the children the story of Purim, all about Esther, the good queen, Ahasueras, the weak king, Haman, the wicked prime minister, and Mordecai who stood up to him. The whole gang couldn't wait to go home, for now they surely knew the meaning of Purim and they would have no trouble at all twirling the groggy Praguer grogger.

Leila was the first to try. "I know the meaning of Purim. Once there was a wicked man named Haman, and he got angry at Mordecai, because Mordecai wouldn't bow down to him, and when he found out Mordecai was Jewish he wanted to kill all the Jews, but what he didn't know was that the King had married this nice Jewish girl named Esther. In fact, even the King didn't know Esther was Jewish or that she was Mordecai's cousin. And when Mordecai found out what was up he told Esther to DO SOMETHING even though she could not even get in to see the King without an invitation, but she went in anyway and he was real nice and said she could have almost anything she wanted (up to half his kingdom) but she said all she wanted was for Haman not to kill her and her people and the King became angry at Haman and hanged him on the gallows he had built for Mordecai and the Jews were saved and that's the meaning of Purim. Now GIMME THAT GROGGER" Leila twirled and twirled but to no avail. It was still a groggy grogger.

Then Lazer said, "I guess that's not what Purim is all about."

"I'm up next," said Penina-Pesha. "I'll tell you what Purim really means. It means that people shouldn't push us Jews around and anytime anybody anywhere tries to make it rough for us, then, like Esther, we should have the guts to stand up for our rights and defend ourselves against all our enemies. That's what Purim's all about: the right of the Jewish people to freedom and peace. Now I'll show you how to twirl a grogger." Penina-Pesha gave it her best effort, but still not a sound.

Finally Charley Braunstein said, "You know, gang, we must be leaving something out. Purim IS about the story of Esther, Mordecai, Ahasuerus and Haman, and Purim sure does mean that we Jews have the right to defend ourselves so we can live in peace.

"But if we Jews should be free from prejudice and persecution so all people should be free. If we Jews have the right to do our own thing without being pushed around, so all other people should have the right to do their thing without being pushed around. I mean bigotry and oppression are wrong no matter who is the victim,"

Then Charley Braunstein twirled the groggy Praguer grogger, and what do you know? The grogger was grogging at last. Lazer said, "So that's what Purim's all about!"

LEILA LEARNS WHAT
THE SEDER IS ALL ABOUT

Charley Braunstein had a brain storm: "Hey, gang, let's have a second seder tonight, just for kids; no grown-ups allowed."

"What a stupid idea," said Leila. "Who's gonna lead it?"

"I will," said Lazer.

SEDER SYMBOLS

"I told you it was a stupid idea," said Leila. But the other kids liked the idea, so on the second night of Pesach the gang went over to Charley's house and had their own seder. They did make some changes. Instead of reading the entire Haggadah, they told the story of the escape from Egypt and explained the symbols with melodies composed by Daniel, who wrote such songs as, "Why, oh why oh why oh; why did we ever leave old Cairo." But the song the kids liked most was written by Charley. They sang it to the tune of "Mother."

M is for the many times I've munched you
A is for your arid after taste
T is for the trouble to digest you
Z is for my zest for bread displaced
O is for the oldest Jewish pastry
S is for your secret recipe
Put them all together they spell Matzos,
Manischewitz' gift to me.

Then Charley became serious and asked: "What do you think is the most important sentence in the Haggadah?"

Lazer answered: "'In each generation every person (not just every Jew but every human being) should see him/her self as though he/she had been brought out of Egypt.' This means to me that we should all imagine what it's like to be a slave."

EGYPTIAN TASKMASTER

"Ridiculous," said Leila. "It's impossible for us to imagine what it's like to be a slave. Let's eat." So they ate, but instead of gefilte fish and chicken, they had pickles and matzaburgers. After the meal it was time to look for the afikomen, which Charley had hidden in the living room where there was a large mirror that his mother called "a looking glass." Leila was so anxious to be the first to find the afikomen that she rushed into the living room and—crash—she went right through the looking glass.

Leila felt herself falling, falling, until she landed with a thud right in the middle of a pile of bricks. All around her people were spreading mortar on the bricks and stacking them one on top of the other. A large man with a whip came toward her. He looked like the picture of the Egyptian in the Haggadah.

"Whatdayathink this is, a school picnic? Don't you know you're a slave. Spread that mortar! Stack those bricks!" And he started whipping Leila.

"I'm spreading. I'm stacking," she cried. When the Egyptian wasn't looking, Leila started running. The Egyptian started chasing her. Leila ran and ran through time and space 'til she dropped from exhaustion . . .

When Leila looked around, she saw to her left a great castle and outside were knights in armor. She realized that somehow she was in the Middle Ages. To her right was a tall brick wall and in the wall was a gate and looking through the gate in the wall Leila could see little houses packed close together and hundreds of people looking through the doors and windows. Leila thought: "How could so many people live in such a small space. They must be miserable."

Then a man dressed in a suit of armor came over to her and said, "Little girl, in Europe in the Middle Ages in many cities, Jews must wear yellow badges and live in ghettos."

"Why?" asked Leila.

"Because said the knight, everybody knows that the Jews poison the wells and make us sick with the Black Plague"

"You're sick, all right," said Leila, "sick in the head," and she started running away. But the knight on his horse started chasing her shouting,

"Where's your yellow badge?" But Leila ran faster and faster through time and space 'til, once again, she collapsed.

When Leila looked around, she was in the middle of a cotton field. She looked at her hands and arms and, for heaven's sake, they had turned dark brown. All around Leila were brown and black people pickin' cotton and this man with a whip (who looked like that knight) came over and said: "Liza, you bettah pick this whole row of cotton or you ain't gettin' no suppah."

Leila looked at the long row of cotton and cried, "My name is Leila, not Liza."

"I don't care what your name is. A *zhid(Jew)* is a *zhid.* If we let you go free, you may go to college, and there won't be any room for us white folks." Leila ran again 'til she collapsed and found herself in a strange land.

"Don't you know you're in Russia," said a man with an accent Leila had never heard. "If you're Jewish that means you're part of a Zionist-imperialist-capitalist conspiracy and belong in jail in Siberia." Leila didn't understand what the man was talking about, so she ran again round and round, 'til suddenly she looked up and saw that she was surrounded by broken glass and all the gang.

"That was some fall you took through Mom's looking glass," said Charley. "You've been knocked out, unconscious for about ten minutes." All Leila could do was blink.

"Let's get back to the seder" said Lazer.

"But nobody has found the afikomen," said Charley. Penina-Pesha helped Leila up, and there on the carpet by the broken mirror was the afikomen.

"Now," said Lazer, "it's time to open the door for Elijah. When we open the door we are praying for the time when all people of every race and religion will be free and at peace."

"AMEN!" shouted Leila. Everybody looked at her with surprise. She kept talking: "We gotta have freedom and peace for all people because, I can tell you, it's horrible to be a slave or to be persecuted or to have people pick on you because of your race or religion."

Charley asked, "How do you suddenly know what it's like to be a slave?

Leila rubbed the bump on her head and said, "Believe me, I know."

LEILA BREAKS A COMMANDMENT

It was almost seven weeks after Passover, and Leila developed this craving for a pocket knife. She asked her mother who said sweetly: "No, Leila dear, pocket knives are for boys."

"Sexist!" cried Leila. "My own mother discriminates against women. All I want to do is to carve a totem pole."

"But you might hurt yourself," said her mother. "How about a nice doll."

"Thanks for nuthin'," Leila said and walked away muttering, "I can take care of myself."

At the pool where Charley, Leila and the gang went swimming there was a life guard called Mack the Knife. His real name was Marvin Mackintosh, but they called him Mack the Knife because he liked to carve little figures out of soap and throw them into the pool and watch them float. One day when Mack had left his chair to break up a fight by the side of the pool, Leila sneaked up to Mack's chair and swiped the knife. She became a *ganiff*, a thief. But as Leila ran home, she didn't feel as though she had done anything wrong. She said to herself: Mack can always buy another knife, but this is the only way I can get one.

Leila hid the knife in the bottom of her dresser drawer. At night she would take it out and see how it gleamed in the light of the moon. Then she found a piece of wood and made a little totem pole, each night carving a different face. One day when Leila's mother was putting some clothes in Leila's drawer, she saw the knife and she was furious. She demanded to know from Leila, "Where did you get that knife?"

"I found it in the woods," Leila lied.

Her mother got red in the face and said: "Wait 'til your father hears about this."

Leila's father was not so strict as her mother and he said: "If she wants a knife so bad, let her keep it." So Leila kept the knife, but she felt a little uncomfortable inside. A few days later she went to the synagogue for Shavuot services. She knew that Shavuot means "weeks," and it falls seven weeks after Passover. She also knew that Reb Hayyim either read or sang the ten commandments. He had many times explained "The freedom the Israelites enjoyed on Passover means nothing unless there are rules to guide the freedom. That's why Shavuot is so important. That's when we read the Ten Commandments which tell us some of the most important rules."

Leila knew all that. She even knew a song that Daniel made up to be sung on Shavuot. For music he used the melody of a folk song called "The Ballad of Jesse James." As she walked to the synagogue on Shavuot, Leila was singing to herself, Daniel's version of the Ten Commandments:

**MOSES & the
TEN COMMANDMENTS**

Moses—he was the man
Who led out of Egypt land
The children of Israel
He didn't use a sword
He just prayed to the Lord
And knew he would not fail.

Chorus: Then Moses climbed the mountain

The people started countin'
Forty nights and days
All alone on the peak
His heart began to speak
And this is what the heart of Moses says:

By word or by deed
You shouldn't worship greed
Or bow before the great God gold
After all is said and done
There is really only One
And that's the God we prayed to of old.
(Oh, Moses climbed the mountain . . . (Chorus)

When you're hot under the collar
You just may want to holler
And raise a lot of cain
Some yellin' is okay
But something we don't say:
Thou shalt not take the Lord's name in vain!

Chorus: Oh, Moses climbed the mountain . . .

If you keep the Shabbat
You better have a lot
Of candles and of wine

And before the main dish
Have some gefilte fish
And you'll be feeling fine.

Chorus: Oh, Moses climbed the mountain . . .

Sometimes you might
Get into a fight with your sister or brother
But never say nay
Love, honor and obey
Your father and your mother.

Chorus: Oh, Moses climbed the mountain . . .

The world has had its fill
Of folks who like to kill
And hurt their fellowman
If wars would only cease
Then we could have peace
In each and every land.

Chorus: Oh, Moses climbed the mountain . . .

Now husbands and wives
If they want to lead good lives
And have a happy home,
Just like birds of a feather
They should have fun together
And never ever roam.

Chorus: Oh, Moses climbed the mountain . . .

If somebody took
Your game or toy or book
Just think how you would feel
That's something no Jew
Or Gentile should do:
Thou shalt never steal

Chorus: Oh, Moses climbed the mountain . . .

You should always beware
Of slander and take care
Of a rumor dressed in red, white and blue
You may get mad at your mommie
But don't call her a commie
Because it isn't true.

Chorus: Oh, Moses climbed the mountain . . .

There are girls and there are fellas
Who are always getting jealous
Of what their neighbors have got
They would feel like millionaires
If they'd value what was theirs
Instead of wanting what they have not.

Chorus: Oh, Moses climbed the mountain . . .

Leila went to services and listened as the Rabbi chanted and someone else translated the Ten Commandments. She paid particular attention to Number Eight, *Lo tignov.* Thou shalt not steal.

After services Leila went to Mack the Knife and gave him his knife and said how sorry she was. She walked home slowly knowing that she had finally done the right thing.

WHAT BAR/BAT MITZVAH IS ALL ABOUT

The time finally came for Charley Braunstein to prepare for becoming a Bar Mitzvah. For a few years he had been attending Hebrew School. But now he was ready to learn to read from the Torah, itself, some story about how Jacob had the craziest dream, something about a ladder that went up to heaven and angels were going up and coming down the ladder.

BAR MITZVAH

But when it was time for Charley's first Torah lesson, he shocked the Rabbi. He shocked his parents. He even shocked the gang by saying: "I don't want to become a Bar Mitzvah!"

"Whadayamean you don't want to be a Bar Mitzvah," shouted his father. "I've already rented the country club."

His mother cried: "I've already sent out the invitations. What'll we tell your Uncle Moishe."

"Sorry," said Charley, "I just don't wanna be a Bar Mitzvah"

"But," said his mother, "all your friends are gonna be Bar or Bat."

Charley replied: "Maybe I should talk to them about it." So the next afternoon just before Hebrew classes, Charley said to the gang, "I don't think I'll go to Hebrew school anymore. I just don't want to be a Bar Mitzvah. Why should I be?"

Linus said: "Every boy in the synagogue becomes a Bar Mitzvah."

Charley answered: "But I'm not every boy."

Leila snapped: "You're sick, Charley Braunstein. Think of the presents; think of the loot: the fountain pens, the hockey sticks, the tennis rackets, the money."

Charley replied: "I get enough presents for my birthday and for Hanukkah."

Daniel was playing Ayn Kelohaynu on the piano but stopped long enough to say: "But Charley, you'll be the star, the center of attention. It will be a great performance. You may even win an Oscar for the best Davener of the Year."

Penina-Pesha added: "And Charley, think of the party, what fun you'll have. They may even make a statue of you out of chopped liver. And think of us. If you don't become a Bar Mitzvah, we'll have one less party this year."

"Sorry," said Charley, "I just don't go for the three p's: the presents, the performance and the party."

Then the whole gang shouted: "Don't you want to be a man!"

Charley started shaking. "N-n-no . . . not yet. I guess that's what scares me more than anything. They keep telling Bar Mitzvahs, 'Today you are a man,' and I'm just not ready."

Then Snappy barked: "Rav, rav, rav," which, of course means: Go to the rav, the Rabbi. So Charley went to Reb Hayyim and told him all his parents had said and all the gang had said and how he just wasn't ready to be a man.

"I see," said the Rabbi. "I don't think you're ready to be man either. But, tell me, do you want to be a child all your life."

"I guess not," said Charley, "not ALL my life."

"So," said the Rabbi, "if you're going to grow from childhood to manhood, the age of thirteen is a pretty good time to start growing."

"A time to start growing from childhood to manhood," said Charley as though to himself.

"That's right," said the Rabbi. "You're not going to become a man overnight. But you're not a little kid anymore either. As a Bar Mitzvah, you're entering kind of an age in between childhood and manhood."

"You mean, Rabbi, I'm becoming an adolescent."

"More or less," said the Rabbi. "In the next few years you'll be finding out what's really special about you . . . what you want to do with your life . . . what you're good at doing and not so good at doing. You'll be discovering your own identity."

"You mean," said Charley, "I won't have to be a copy of anybody else, so I can be an original."

"You got it," said the Rabbi. "This is the time you should have faith, faith in your own God-given power to grow, a time to believe that whatever problems lie ahead, you can overcome them."

"Well," said Charley," those ideas make sense. I don't feel grown up; I don't feel like a man, but I do want to be one."

"By the way," said the Rabbi. "At the age of thirteen, you're not yet a man, and there's something else you're not yet."

"What's that?" asked Charley.

"You're not yet an adult Jew. You don't yet know what Judaism is all about."

"That's for sure," said Charley. "I haven't really learned that much in Hebrew School."

"I know," said the Rabbi. "Judaism is really a religion for grownup minds. And it's just impossible to understand the ideas of our religion when you're still a child. That's why it's so important to learn about an adult Judaism in the years when you're growing to manhood."

Charley asked: "Are you telling me that if I don't learn more about Judaism, I'll be living as an adult with the religion of a thirteen year old.?

"Right!" said the Rabbi "That is known as Bar Mitzvah fixation: when you grow in many ways but Jewishly you are fixated, stuck at a pre-adolescent understanding of your religion."

"You mean," said Charley," Bar Mitzvah means I'm not only growing toward manhood but I'm also taking a step toward a grown-up knowledge of Judaism."

"Well put," said the Rabbi. "Now you know what the Mitzvah in Bar Mitzvah means: Thou shalt grow into a mature knowledgeable Jew."

"Okay, Rabbi," said Charley, "I guess it's time I start growing up."

The Rabbi smiled and said: "That's great, Charley. You know, girls also have to grow up. That's why a girl becomes a Bat Mitzvah, a daughter of the commandment."

BAT MITZVAH

"You mean," asked Charley, "it's just as important for Jewish girls to understand their religion as it is for boys?"

"That's right," said the Rabbi. "Now there was this teen-ager named Jacob, and he had this crazy dream about a ladder . . ."

ISRAEL'S RIGHT TO BE

One day in the middle of May, Leila came home from school with a black eye. "What happened?" asked Charley.

"I went to school wearing a star of David in honor of Israel's anniversary and some kid said, 'Death to Israel!' I didn't know how to answer him so I socked him and he socked me."

'But why would anyone say, 'Death to Israel,'" asked Charley. "We better ask Reb Hayyim. He'll have an answer."

So the gang went to see the Rabbi, and he smiled sadly and said, "There are some people who don't believe that Israel has a right to exist as a homeland for the Jewish people."

"But almost every other people has a homeland," interjected Charley.

"It's more complicated," said the Rabbi. Except for the time when the Jews were exiled to Babylon (586 BCE-538 BCE) most of the Jews lived in Palestine for almost 1400 years. Then the Romans drove all but a small minority out. (There was over the years a small group of Jews in Palestine; in the 16th century, Jewish mysticism flourished.) But they never regained independence.

"You have all heard of the Holocaust when Hitler killed about six million Jews. Still several hundred thousand escaped, but no country, not even the U.S.A., would take them all in. Most wanted to return to Palestine. That's where the Jewish people had lived longer than any other people under one God."

"That's where the prophets preached about justice and peace. That's the land to which the Jews had prayed one day to return. For centuries the Jews prayed that the messiah would appear and lead them back to Palestine. But in the late 19h century, Zionist leaders, such as Herzl. argued that the Jewish people could not wait for the messiah. They developed Zionist leaders whose purpose was to re-establish a Jewish state in Palestine."

"So what's the problem?" asked Charley.

"You have to understand that about 1300 years ago the Arabs moved into Palestine, so they claimed the land as their own."

"But," Charley asked, "why didn't the Arabs set up their own state in Palestine."

"One reason," said the Rabbi "is that the Arabs in Palestine did not feel a sense of Palestinian identity until after the first World War when they were under the British mandate."

"Why didn't they divide the land?" asked Daniel.

"That's what the United Nations decided to do in November, 1947. After the British left in May, 1948, the UN said the land should be divided: one part for the Jewish people; another part for the Arabs who considered themselves Palestinians. But the Palestinians rejected the partition plan and attacked the Jews living there. There was a bloody war. The Jews won and even captured more territory than the UN proposed they have, and that is how Israel was born."

"So why didn't they just make peace, like happens after most wars?" asked Charley.

Reb Hayyim answered: "Thousands of Arabs fled the land during the war to get away from the fighting. Some were pushed out by the Israelis. They demanded the right to return. Some settled in land the UN wanted to be a Palestinian state: some on the West Bank of the Jordan; others down south in Gaza. The surrounding Arab states would not accept them as citizens. So they thought of themselves as refugees. Meanwhile thousands of Jews had moved to Israel from Arab countries, and they were accepted as citizens"

"But," interrupted Leila, "the Palestinians wouldn't have refugees if they had accepted the UN's two state solution."

"True," said the Rabbi, "but most of them believed the Jews had no right to any state in Palestine. They thought the entire Middle-East belonged to the Arabs."

"This is getting too complicated," said Lazer. "Can't you talk about what's happening now?"

"Well," said the Rabbi. "I'll make it brief. In 1967, Egypt and Syria threatened to destroy Israel, but the Israelis struck first, and in six days destroyed the Egyptian air force and occupied the West Bank and Gaza. The Arabs refused to accept Israel's offer to return the occupied territory in return for a permanent peace. Since 1969, there has been fighting between the two peoples but also attempts at achieving peace. Some Israelis built settlements on land that the UN said should go to the Arabs. They thought that would make them safer, but they made the Arabs even angrier. Finally the Israelis withdrew their settlements in Gaza, but extremist Arabs called Hamas took over and started sending rockets into Israel. The Israelis fought back."

"So is there no hope?" asked Charley.

"There is always hope," said the Rabbi. "That's the name of the Israeli national anthem, 'HaTikvah,' 'the hope.' Daniel began playing HaTikvah on the piano. "Many Palestinians on the West Bank of the Jordan want to make peace and there are even now efforts to come to some compromise. Our own country, the USA supports the 'two-state solution.' But it won't be easy. Palestinians living in Israel don't want to move to a Palestinian state. Israelis living in the West Bank don't want to leave."

Charley interrupted: "Why shouldn't the Palestinians in Israel stay where they are, and why shouldn't some Israelis stay on the West Bank in exchange for territory that Israel would give to the Palestinians?"

"Maybe you should be a diplomat," said the Rabbi to Charley.

Leila complained, "You haven't told me what to say to those kids who say 'Death to Israel.'"

The Rabbi answered: "Just tell them that both peoples have a right to part of the land and they should live in peace. As Micah said a long time ago, 'Let everyone live under his vine and fig tree and let no one be afraid.'"

JERUSALEM

ISRAEL